THE SCULPTURE OF
GASTON LACHAISE

THE SCULPTURE OF
GASTON LACHAISE

WITH AN ESSAY BY

Hilton Kramer

AND APPRECIATIONS BY

Hart Crane, E. E. Cummings, Marsden Hartley

Lincoln Kirstein, A. Hyatt Mayor

& Henry McBride

THE EAKINS PRESS PUBLISHERS NEW YORK

ACKNOWLEDGMENTS

THANKS ARE DUE to Professor Donald B. Goodall, Chairman of the Department of Art of the University of Texas, whose research has established the dates of various events in the life of Lachaise and the period of many undated works. Mr. Goodall is preparing a *catalogue raisonné* and a study of the artist's work. The research of Mr. Gerald Nordland, director of the San Francisco Museum of Art and the author of a recent essay on Lachaise, has also been relied upon.

The publishers wish to express their appreciation for the cooperation of Mr. Donald Gallup of the Yale University Library, Miss Antoinette Kraushaar of the Kraushaar Galleries, Miss Margaret McKellar and Mrs. Patricia Fitzgerald Mandel of The Whitney Museum of American Art, and Miss Pearl Moeller of The Museum of Modern Art. Miss Ruth Hokanson was responsible for editorial research, and Miss Elizabeth Oppenheimer and Mr. Howard Rogovin were of assistance in making special arrangements for photographs. Many of the photographs were made especially for this publication by Mr. John D. Schiff.

Grateful acknowledgment is due museums and individual collectors who have kindly allowed works in their possession to be reproduced.

Mr. Felix Landau of the Felix Landau Gallery, Los Angeles, made valuable suggestions for the book in connection with a series of exhibitions of certain works of Lachaise presently being planned for selected museums throughout the country.

This first volume on the life-work of Lachaise is in large measure the result of the initiative, interest and support of the Managing Trustee of the Lachaise Foundation, Mr. John B. Pierce, Jr., of Boston, Massachusetts.

The contents have been selected and edited by Mr. Leslie Katz and Mr. Robert J. Schoelkopf, Jr.

CONTENTS

GASTON LACHAISE
by Hilton Kramer

IN THE HISTORY of modern sculpture the art of Gaston Lachaise occupies an important but an anomalous position. A great sculptor Lachaise undoubtedly was, but among his peers in this century he is one of the most difficult to place with any finality, for his work embraces two worlds and its characteristic realization bears the mark of their collision. To grasp the full significance of this sculpture, to see the ways in which the artist joined the heritage of one world with the peculiar pressures of the other and thus converted a potentially disruptive history into an art of remarkable originality, consistency, and force, it is essential to see the work itself in the context of the drama that produced it. Though, like all great art, Lachaise's ultimately stands free of both biography and history, our understanding of his work is considerably enhanced by some knowledge of the way he came to create it.

Lachaise was born in Paris, in 1882, and was apparently committed to his vocation at an early age. He was trained while still a youth at the École Bernard Palissy and the Académie Nationale des Beaux-Arts. In all matters of craft and artisanship, and in the tenor of the sensibility that governed them, he was French. As a mature artist he had at his fingertips all the refinement and facility of technique that were once the glory of the great European art academies. Yet the maturity of his art belongs to America. It was in America that his art first came to flower. It was under the pressure of his American experience that Lachaise developed his own extraordinary vision and came to produce a sculptural *oeuvre* that resembles no other on either side of the Atlantic.

What brought Lachaise to America was an encounter, while still in Paris, that changed the course of his life. "At twenty, in Paris," he later wrote, "I met a young American person who immediately became the primary inspiration which awakened my vision and the leading influence that has directed my

9

forces." This "young American person" was Isabel Nagle, the Bostonian lady whom Lachaise followed to America and later made his wife. It was she who became his model, his muse, and his abiding inspiration. Virtually all of Lachaise's greatest work is an attempt to encompass and to celebrate the force she represented in his life. Both the eroticism and the monumentality of his art, and especially their combination in certain works that have still not lost their power to shock, owe a great deal to the peculiar rapture this "young American person" sustained in Lachaise's life to the very end.

But it is not out of rapture alone, of course, that an artist fashions his work. If, as a man, Lachaise was in thrall to this woman to an unusual degree—unusual insofar as he made that thralldom the central emotion of his art—he was, as a sculptor, none the less a man of his time. And his sculpture developed out of a tradition only recently revived in France when he undertook his initial training—the tradition of the heroic figure redeemed by Rodin and his followers from the decline that had overtaken it several centuries earlier. In the end Lachaise's art bursts the boundaries implicitly defined by this revival, and joins in the aesthetic adventure of those who reacted against the Rodin standard. But the beginnings of his art are to be found at the juncture where his finical Beaux-Arts training and the exalted ambitions of Rodin meet and fertilize each other.

Lachaise came to America in 1906, shortly before his twenty-fourth birthday. Though he once described the period—it appears to have been several years—between Isabel Nagle's return to Boston and his own departure from Paris as time spent "lazily contemplating masterpieces of the past," he had in fact already entered into the art life of a gifted Beaux-Arts student, showing his work each year in the Salon des Artistes Français and competing for the coveted Prix de Rome. But at some point, probably early in 1905, he interrupted his career to take a job doing precision work for a famous jeweler, René Lalique, in order to secure money for the trip to America. (It was the first of many such interruptions that lack of money would force upon Lachaise, though in later years the sums he felt were needed to keep himself and his beloved Isabel were often sizable indeed.) He arrived in Boston on January 13, 1906, with thirty dollars in his pocket—a sculptor by ambition, a craftsman by trade, a passionate and romantic foreigner, unable to speak a word of English, his mind filled with the poetry of Baudelaire, Verlaine, and Rimbaud, and in feverish pursuit of a mistress (herself a married woman with a child) ten years his senior.

Lachaise worked, first in Boston and then in New York, in the workshops of academic sculptors—first Henry Hudson Kitson and then Paul Manship—who were at that time the steady recipients of highly lucrative public commissions. But Lachaise demonstrated from the very start of his new life in America that he was a man—and an artist—of prodigious energy and ambition, with a sense of vocation that far transcended his immediate workaday circumstances. His first major work, the great *Standing Woman*, also known as *Elevation* (1912—1927, 70 inches high), was begun in his room in Washington Square the year he moved to New York. Like the other sculpture he showed in his first one-man exhibition at the Stephan Bourgeois Gallery in February 1918—on that occasion, the *Standing Woman* was shown in plaster —it was executed in the few hours a night left to Lachaise after a full day's work on Manship's monuments. By 1913, Isabel Nagle had joined him in New York, and they were soon married. It was then that his career began in earnest, and he worked like a man doubly possessed.

The cultural circumstances of the time—a time when modernism in all the arts was the taste of the very few, and philistinism still reigned undisturbed in high places—precluded the possibility that Lachaise would meet with widespread approval or gain a large following. But he was fortunate in winning early recognition from the small circle of artists and connoisseurs who knew the modern movement in Europe at firsthand and perceived Lachaise's distinction virtually on contact. Through a chance encounter with Arthur B. Davies in Kitson's studio, one of Lachaise's sculptures was included in the Armory Show of 1913—a plaster *Nude With Coat* (circa 1912, 10¾ inches high). His two exhibitions at the Bourgeois Gallery—the second came in 1920 —were enthusiastically praised by Henry McBride, the most informed American critic of the period. And the twenties saw Lachaise become a sort of sculptor laureate of *The Dial*, whose publishers, Scofield Thayer and James Sibley Watson, not only published illustrations of his work (beginning with their first number) and numerous articles about him but also commissioned many of the portrait heads that form a portion of his *oeuvre* only second in importance to his female nudes. Throughout his life—Lachaise died in 1935, just after Lincoln Kirstein organized a retrospective exhibition of his work at the Muse-

11

um of Modern Art—he enjoyed the esteem of New York's intellectual and artistic elite. Distinguished galleries showed him, and distinguished critics lavished intelligent attention on his work. If he did not die a great success in worldly terms—and McBride's memorable obituary in the *Sun* is sufficient reminder that he did not—it was only because America itself was not yet willing to grant an achievement of his quality and originality a high place in the scheme of worldly values.

From the beginning of his work in America, Lachaise adopted two modes of sculptural discourse—one public and monumental, in which an avowal of private emotion is transmuted into a rhetoric of almost archetypal universality and impersonality; and the other, highly personal and intimate, in which fantasy stimulated by private passion is made to yield a vocabulary of forms of breathtaking candor and invention. The one reminds us of Lachaise's creative relation to the line that joins the highly expressive classicism of Rodin to the abstract purity of Brancusi; the other underscores Lachaise's daring in joining this line with sources—in Indian, archaic, primitive and prehistoric sculpture —that enabled him to realize a range of erotic imagery not to be found in conventions nearer at hand.

Of his monumental works, three are pre-eminent: the *Standing Woman* (*Elevation*), already mentioned; *Floating Figure* (1927), 51¾ by 96 inches long; and the *Standing Woman* (1932), 88 inches high, whose commanding position in the garden of the Museum of Modern Art has established it as one of the most familiar of modern classics. Each is a quite different conception, but all three are characterized by an astonishing robustness and serenity, by an immense weightiness and massiveness elevated to a lyric *calme et volupté*.

In the first, the handsomely endowed nude figure is given a delicate but emphatic upward movement—hence, presumably, the title *Elevation*, given it by Stephan Bourgeois. The entire form is invested with a single, beautifully contained gesture, suggesting at once a memory of erotic transport and something more spiritual, detached, and classic. The exquisitely varied masses— rising from the narrow, graceful feet on tiptoe to the musculature of the pronounced thighs and torso to the elegant arms that are carried, rather like a dancer's, to understated points of climax in the poetry of the hands—are a miracle of modeling in which we see Lachaise's profound technical power here imbued for the first time with his quest for a heroic image.

12

There is already more than a hint in this piece that such a quest could not, in Lachaise's case, be satisfied without recourse to a sculptural grammar more radical in its amplifications and exaggerations than any to be found in his immediate predecessors or contemporaries. By the time he came to make the *Floating Woman* of 1927, this radical grammar was very far advanced. The breasts, the abdomen, the thighs, the buttocks—upon each of these elements the sculptor lavishes a powerful and incisive massiveness, a rounded voluminousness, that answers not to the descriptions of nature but to an ideal prescribed by his own emotions. And in all three of these monumental works, there is an ideality that saves them from the grossness Lachaise seemed eager to risk—a grossness that did overtake such works as *Man* (1930), a male nude 100 inches in height, and *"Dans La Nuit"* (1935, 88½ by 41 inches), an audacious depiction of reclining lovers. The *Floating Woman* does indeed float. There is no exaggeration in the extravagant parts that is not equilibrated in the transcendent economy and tranquility of the whole. Where Lachaise is in complete command of his powers, as he is in this work, its very exaggerations of weight and form contribute to its essential buoyancy.

In the *Standing Woman* of 1932, it is the reverse of buoyancy that is sought. This is a triumphant figure of earth. Its stance is at once forthright and detached, open and immovable. Its silhouette has an elegant, vital force, and its idealized anatomy, with its undulating rhythm of a clearly defined plasticity, is endowed with an elemental power. The feet are firm on their pedestal; the grip of the hands, on hip and thigh, is unhesitating; the thrust of the belly—itself one of the most beautiful forms in modern sculpture—utterly imperious. The neck supporting its goddesslike head is a statement of immutable strength. Nowhere in Lachaise's *oeuvre* is his favored conception of the female figure—with the breasts and arms, the thighs and buttocks and belly forming a centrifugal orchestration of masses around the delicate, slender waist—given a more complete realization.

It was Lachaise's distinction to sustain this mode of sculptural discourse with an exemplary dignity and splendor, and at a time when there were virtually no precedents and certainly no official encouragements in this country for a public art on this level. No doubt his European background acted as a shield against the parochial values that dominated American sculpture in his lifetime.

13

The *Standing Woman* of 1932 is, in my view, the central ornament of Lachaise's achievement, a work that can stand beside the greatest works of the century. But it does not, in itself, give us a complete revelation of Lachaise's gifts and of his inordinate obsessions as an artist. For that, one must look to the series of small figures and fragments of figures in which he displayed his emotions more openly, his virtuosity as a modeler more variously, and the extremes of his invention more candidly.

He was a master modeler from the start. The small upright female figures in various stages of undress that Lachaise produced from 1910 to the early twenties are wonderfully observed studies from the model, *his* model, in which the expressive properties of the modeling process itself are at times given an importance equal to that of the subject. Where he refined and simplified these studies, we already have a glimpse of his monumental mode, and there are works among them—particularly, the superlative "*La Force Eternelle*" (1917), a sculpture that always calls to mind Baudelaire's *Les Bijoux*—that would have made handsome life-size sculpture.

But beautiful as these earlier small figures are, it is not in them that one feels Lachaise reaching the heights of his expressive powers. The poses tend to rehearse the familiar standing position, and it was not until Lachaise subjected the figure to unorthodox postures (bordering at times on the grotesque), or fragmented the figure either for the purpose of abstract refinement (as in the elegant *Torso* of 1930), or in order to distort certain portions of the anatomy to an expressive extreme (as in the magnified treatment of the breasts in the *Torso* of 1928), or else isolated parts of the anatomy altogether, that the breadth of the sculptor's invention was fully engaged. It is in this (mainly later) work that we see the pressure of Lachaise's erotic fantasy yielding a truly amazing variety of sculptural ideas and realizations.

For what is notable about Lachaise's fragmentation of the figure is the degree to which he carried it. Rodin, of course, had made partial figures and fragments of figures, as had his followers; the practice became an established convention under his influence. But Lachaise's tendency to amplify and exaggerate those parts of the female anatomy that most excited his fancy—by which one means his sculptural sensibility quite as much as his erotic susceptibility—resulted in a style that treated the fragment as a discrete and total object on its own. Neither the *Torso* of 1930, with its Brancusian refinement

14

and simplification, nor the equally refined marble *Knees* of 1933 nor the fantastic *Torso with Arms Raised* of 1935 nor the sensational *Breasts with Female Organ Between* of 1930–1932 is intended as a substitute for or reminiscence of the complete figure. There is no suggestion of a ruin; we are not left contemplating anything partial or severed from an ideal whole. Indeed, it is not to the convention of Rodin that one turns for the closest comparison but to Brancusi, not only because of the works (already cited) in which Lachaise seemed actually to draw closer to Brancusi's example but because even at the opposite pole of expression, where Lachaise lavished all his energy on treating a particular motif with an extravagant superrealism, he conceived its sculptural realization in terms of a completely contained formal statement.

Had Lachaise lived a longer life, he would undoubtedly have carried his exploration of these close-up views of the female anatomy, together with his interest in unorthodox poses, to a new synthesis of the figure. As it was, he did produce one stunning work—the *"Dynamo Mother"* of 1933—in which the abundant female figure is situated in a posture of birth which is at the same time a posture of love, with limbs radically foreshortened and sexual organs enlarged, and the entire sculptural mass modeled to convey a surpassing sense of erotic vitality.

It is as a sculptor of the female nude that Lachaise makes the most imperative claim on our attention, but this was not the only work that occupied him. His portrait heads alone would have earned him an independent fame had he produced nothing else. At their best—as in the portraits of John Marin, Henry McBride, Edgard Varèse, and the young Timothy Seldes—they occupy a place just after Rodin but before Epstein in the quality of their realization, in the way Lachaise was able to transmute a likeness into a sculptural structure of complete integrity. Some of Lachaise's portraits are, to be sure, of a rather perfunctory nature, but there is always something in them—quite apart from the record they offer of the leading personalities of a great period in the cultural life of New York—to sustain our interest. And beside the portrait heads, there are several extraordinary full-length nude male portrait figures—the outstanding example being the *Boy with a Tennis Racket* (1933). Clearly the male figure did not engage Lachaise's interest with anything like the intensity he brought to the female form, but in these few nude male portraits his fidelity to observed fact acted as an effective brake against the tendency to ponderous idealization that sometimes compromised his more monumental male nudes.

And then there are the numerous decorative objects Lachaise produced—the exquisite dolphins and birds and other sculptural fauna that the artisan in Lachaise seemed to produce in almost effortless profusion and that the artist in him always touched with an elegant poetry. They are sometimes slight, and never profound; but they bear the mark of a first-rate sensibility.

Where, then, does this varied accomplishment place Lachaise in the sculpture of his time?

In the American sculpture of his period he is pre-eminent, the only artist in the sculptural medium who, through both the quality and the copiousness of his production, comes in on the level of the great European masters and sustains serious comparison with their best efforts. But even in that company, he eludes a fixed position. One's first inclination is to place him among the votaries of the classical nude—with Rodin, Renoir, and Maillol—yet he seems too modern, too willful, too individual in his vision of the sculptural object to rest easily among them. His intensity disrupts the atmosphere; his radicalism seems to mock their nostalgia.

What one sees in Lachaise's art is a remnant of this classical sensibility provoked and unsettled by the pressure of emotions that far exceed the boundaries of the classical ideal. In producing an art that would be faithful to those emotions, Lachaise actually drew closer to the antagonists of the tradition that nurtured him, and had perforce to look outside that tradition for the precedents he needed to sustain his vision. In this respect, he acted as other votaries of modernist disruption acted, and, like them, he left the art he practiced permanently altered. In Lachaise the mold of the classical tradition is broken—broken, one may say, by a sense of life too forceful and too confident, too unbounded, to contain it.

1967

16

DRAWINGS

TOP 1906–1910. Black Ink and Brush, 9⅝x7¾ inches. Lachaise Foundation.
BOTTOM 1932. Pencil and Blue Ink, 24x19 inches. Lachaise Foundation.

Circa 1930, Pencil Drawing, 24x18⅞ inches. Lachaise Foundation.

1933. Pencil and Blue Ink, 24x19 inches. Lachaise Foundation.

Circa 1934. Ink Drawing, 23⅝ x 18⅝ inches. Lachaise Foundation.

APPRECIATIONS

AN ESSAY BY

E. E. CUMMINGS

From *Creative Art Magazine*, August 1928

THE SOLITUDE called sculpture, of Lachaise, does not date; never describes; cannot pretend. Once within its clutch, we everywhere encounter nothing archaic, nothing modern, nothing unexperienced—everywhere we find ourselves conjugated by a mind which feels freely. By freely, we would infer that to Lachaise any likeness and any abstraction equally are *of*; that keenly his least melody, implacably his hugest rhythm, solves the aesthetic problem of truth; to annihilate *of* through IS.

Take, for example, this face reflecting the spectator; a robust hugeness, beheaded repose, the closing of all lines—a vitality so unmitigated as to become invisible, an almost impertinent fulfillment, supreme luxury of fruition. Pass to these five or six figures, not motion because movement, antitheses of imitation, neither adjectival nor adverbial, unmodifying, actual, not real, distinct, sufficient, reflexive—the one self reddish golden, the other self black; this tumbles, that sprints; another (asquirm, fused) lustily upspouts, innumerably answering the spiral question of mortality. Contrast with a focussed and brutal and centrifugal sexually idiom, sprawled yet flying, one gradual collocation of breasts and thighs, one single effortless glide of volume or faultlessly promulgating structure.

Note next the youth, revealed by more modeling than has existed since Cezanne; compare him with these women—the first erect, a simultaneously buoyant and huge thrust of fifteen vertical inches—the second reclining, a fluent dignity comprised by ceaseless interplay of weights and sizes, an alert fugue of accurate wheres and careful hows—the third seated, invincible idiom of counterpoint, solid as nightmare. Plunge now into that heroic, orchestral *Elevation*; feast on swift masses poised against their own silence (what irreproachable goals of form!) before which we are breathless since it, they, breathes, breathe, so entirely, miraculously. (Indeed, time is that imperfection

25

of ourselves which deludes us into thinking that "life" exists; whereas, among these aesthetic integers, we know that "life" persists merely, or until it dissolves—does not exist at all—in fact perishes.)

Here a head holds, thorough, dense, vigorous; another lives, female, taciturn, an inwardly outwardness; but a third sleeps, fundamental as some piece of driftwood which had used a thousand tides in order simply to become itself. Finally and first, what human or inhuman aspect beckons as intensely as the vast creature, weightless but resolute, in whom we experience not flesh and not form but idea; dreamlike, authentically impossible?

Or let us believe again; believe that once the world was a sea floor; that once ourselves inhabited a sea. Gradually we begin to recognize the pulse of that sea, the texture of our heritage—begin to understand, within the timeful defeat of reality, a timeless triumph of dream. Has not art always kept and remembered, shall it not always give and prophesy? Only and continually the artist has been and will be and is aware through every direction, of unnameable dimensions. If, therefore, the artist creates, it is with these dimensions— and let criticism do its stumbling worst. In the case of Lachaise, before one has spoken one has been already ashamed.

Yet not to speak would be still more shameful; since what matters is that this originator of solitude, called (for lack of a better word) sculpture, should have his chance and day among us. The man through whose touch a few cubic inches become colossal, must fill New York's noisiest corner with silence. To him alone may be entrusted the task of reinventing America's parks, playgrounds, sanctuaries. For a million times a million ofs, a million times a million mendacities, insipidities, and trivialities, Lachaise—by virtue of his freely feeling mind—can exchange the enormous truth. Nor is this our vision so much as our prayer; when imbecility jostles, when ugliness clutters and the world is too much with us, let the ocean of his genius make another sea floor!

MARSDEN HARTLEY

Twice a Year, Fall-Winter 1939

L ACHAISE was that singular being of today and of yesterday, the worshipper of beauty, he thought of nothing else, beauty was his meat and bread, it was his breath and his music, it was the image that traversed his dreams, and troubled his sleep, it was his vital and immortal energy.

Lachaise was unquestionably the true artist, he was the sculptor of the joyous moment, there are, at least not in the major portion of Lachaise's production, no dark and ponderous images in the work of this man, and since for him the dream was a magnificent "affair du coeur" he believed first and last in the efficacy of it, and the proud substance of beauty as a force in itself.

He never was ashamed of using this word for he was a natural male, therefore his notion of the meaning of this element was normal and robust, it was in fact a kind of pontifical high mass for Lachaise, since he was always the consistent and ardent worshipper, he was always at work day and night, sleeping when the body could no longer hold out and above all this ritualist solemnity rises the figure of the indomitable pagan who saw the entire universe in the form of a woman.

The woman who was to supply the completeness of this image was Isabel Dutaud of Cambridge, Massachusetts, born of French parentage, and from the moment of meeting before some amazing object or other thirty years ago in the Musée de Cluny in Paris, these two persons perfectly ordained for each other were joined forever and from this moment on were never to be separated, thirty years of unalloyed happiness and devotion, and so it was that when Gaston Lachaise found Isabel Dutaud he proceeded to love her, work for her, idolize her, glorify her, resting completely immersed in the enveloping warmth of her abundant nature, and from the first moment onward therefore had no thought for or interest in any other single individual. Two things therefore engrossed Lachaise, the one supplied the strength for the other, and these were love and labour, he was indefatigable in his ardour for both these ideas, and fulfilled them to the last.

And because Lachaise worked too terrifically and with unreasoning violence there is every reasonable notion to believe that he destroyed all of his recuperative energies, for at the early age of fifty-two much too early indeed, Lachaise had ceased to function.

Lachaise believed in the grandeur of self-expression above all things and would have agreed with Eva Gauthier who said to me one day when we were talking of the artist's lot, that after all the artist is better off than those who cannot express themselves, and as a sculptor he was much like Maillol and Renoir too, reserving for his special adoration the female form and the symbol of woman in relation to man.

Lachaise was a big man, of better than medium height, dark eyes, dark flowing hair, and an elemental animalistic burning in him like flames on the hilltop of a burning city, you felt the tumult of his ardours and his idealistic ideas in every look and movement of him, he was alive with passion for art and the pure expression of it, he was inordinately simple as well, like a child yet in no way childish, he believed in his personal star and to him it was the most radiant of all, and he left the world outside himself to its own ridiculous or sublime devices, and it mattered not at all which it was.

Lachaise was enclosed in the microcosm of his vision, and was one of the happiest of men, since nothing but joy and the idealist's fervor of living shines out of his work.

He was never victim of that awful impulse in sculptors to symbolize the philosophical depth of things, he could never have done a huge hulk of a male figure with hands on chin and called it "Penseur," never in the world of art, or in any other world, for he would not be thinking like that.

Maillol is perhaps Lachaise's happiest relation in the world of sculpture, they felt so intensely the same sort of idea about woman, just as Renoir was at his best in painting the forms of woman, it is the flesh itself that seems to dynamize such men to idealistic action, and they were all natural males.

Lachaise was more the lyrical histrionist in a way, since nearly all of his female figures assert if not quite dramatize many moods in the same woman, all of his figures are the expression of the immediacy of emotion and of mood, his line is as brilliant as that of Raphael in so many instances and is less hampered by the desire for classical imitation.

He was somewhat also the jeweler in the fashion of Cellini, and if he did not build up his ideas by extraneous ornamentation, he gave them the pressure of swift movement according to the direct states of assertion, and for this reason if for no other the sculpture of Lachaise is always alive and pulsating with life, for the simplest of reasons that he himself was always so.

Lachaise followed his aesthetic demon like a true artist and this demon was perfection, ideality, the reality of ideal experience in life first of all, and through this principle, in his work.

The complete lack of introversion in Lachaise's sculpture gave his work that freshness which is rare especially in sculpture, when the tendency so often is to symbolize and dramatize.

Lachaise hated obliqueness and opacity in matters of art, he was, esthetically speaking, a devout rebel and was emphatically against all that interfered with pure experience, all that partook of the element of pastiche was poison to his eye and spirit.

Whitman speaks somewhere of universal and eternal rondures, and this was the subconscious belief of Lachaise also, he was a romantic poet besides, a kind of lyric architect of the human form.

A POEM BY

HART CRANE

From a letter to Lachaise, January 1924

INTERLUDIUM

Thy time is thee to wend
with languor such as gains
immensity in gathering grace; the arms
to spread; the hands to yield their shells

and fostering
thyself, bestow to thee
illimitable and unresigned
(no instinct flattering vainly now)

thyself that heavens climb to measure
thus unfurling thee untried,—until
from sleep forbidden now
and wide partitions in thee—goes

communicant and speeding new
the cup again wide from thy throat to spend
those streams and slopes untenanted thou
hast known. . . . . And blithe

Madonna, natal to thy yielding
still subsist I, wondrous as
from thy apart dugs shall still the sun
again round one more fairest day. . . . .

LINCOLN KIRSTEIN

Catalogue: Gaston Lachaise, Retrospective Exhibition,
The Museum of Modern Art, January 1935

LACHAISE, above all other sculptors since the Renaissance, is the interpreter of maturity. He is concerned with forms which have completed their growth, which have achieved their prime; forms, as he would say, in the glory of their fulfillment. Amplitude and abundance are not in themselves concepts unpleasing to most people, so long as the expression of them in sculpture is not far removed from a young Greek girl banked with a flowering cornucopia representing Plenty. Acceptance of the idea of maturity today would imply a change in popular psychology. It is no wonder that to a nation predominantly adolescent Lachaise's insistence upon the mature is frightening.

Considered a violent offender against rules of good taste in sculpture, Lachaise can nevertheless rely on many witnesses from the past in art to justify him, should he need them. Michelangelo, Titian, Dürer, Rubens, Rembrandt, Courbet come easily to mind. He feels that he is a link in the tradition of the handling of developed forms, but far more as a re-creation than as a reminiscence of previous epochs. His preferences in the art of the past illuminate his present activity. The past he loves best is remotest, the very earliest dawn of European culture when men inscribed tusked mammoths and bisons on the walls of their stone caverns, beasts with shaggy mountainous bodies delicately balanced on small, careful hoofs. Or small paleolithic objects carved from ivory or stone, female bodies of refined grossness, with huge mounded breasts capable of suckling whole tribes; earth-goddesses which were in ten thousand years to be corrupted into the softer, many-breasted Diana of the Ephesians. Next, he admires the clarity, precision, and anonymity of the Egyptian stone carvers, craftsmen who were capable of taking human models, priest or king, and elevating them into godhead, the cut stone becoming not only a portrait but an expressed fragment of divine vitality, an idol worthy of worship. Lastly he

31

feels himself close to the Hindu sculptors of India and the Malay archipelagos, who allowed themselves great freedom with the human body, adopting hieratic rearrangement and refinement to produce interlocking friezes of terrible dances and scenes of loving and destructive gods. He feels that the cavemen had already all the reverence, simplicity and fervor of subsequent "great" periods, that their painting too had a majesty never revived in later inventions. He admires the force of barbarians and feels there is not nearly enough of their directed impulse in art today. He feels that his own work has a barbarian impulse which, taking nature as its base, makes nature idol-like or godlike. For the well-achieved work of other more civilized periods he has the good craftsman's respect for good craftsmanship. But that is about all. He thinks, for example, that Negro sculpture, considering its conditioning in fear, magic and ceremonial aims, is far more relevant to Africa and to ourselves than is Greek sculpture of the middle or late periods and the decadence of classic traditionalism in the West. A simple, unbiased vision has been difficult for the paler European. He believes that Renaissance imitation of Greek ideals and its various mutations down to our own time are without much inherent energy and in the last analysis only well-executed imitations of a reality far more moving in the flesh. The cavemen knew as much about the relationship of animals to natural forces as contemporary artists despite their advantage of the whole realm of scientific research and developed cosmologies. Not that Lachaise would stop at the mammoth. Only, he would share the grandeur and inevitability of the earlier impulsive awe, unfettered by secondary considerations of decoration or surface refinement or a preconceived idea of what is fitting or beautiful.

A. HYATT MAYOR

From *Hound & Horn*, July–September 1932

PROBABLY no artist now working in this country is more generally misunderstood than Gaston Lachaise. His refusal to join any societies or to subscribe to the catchwords of any clique has isolated him in misapprehension.

To some people his nudes have seemed laden with grossness, though anyone who looks can see that their flesh is not debased, but as buoyant as a Gupta sculpture or the frescoes at Ajanta. And his small bronzes of parts of nudes turning handsprings have looked like mere freakishness. Yet no artist more eagerly embraces restrictions than Lachaise, or feels his inventiveness more stimulated by exact specifications. He is delighted to be bound down to making a relief on a given subject for a particular place and lighting, or to making a faithful likeness of any given horse or man. Many of the small bronzes are "freakish" simply because in making them Lachaise had to invent his own restrictions—had to invent the riddle as well as the answer to the riddle. And being a man of enterprise, he set himself the most intricate riddles he could devise. It is almost too much to ask of an artist that he invent his own problems. They should be imposed by the purpose for which the work is called into being. If Lachaise sometimes seems freakish, it is not because he is wayward, but because his strength has so few exact tasks laid upon it. If he had the glamour of a Paris studio, instead of the commonplace accessibility of Eighth Street, his wits would probably be given enough commands to wrestle with.

Lachaise may have inherited his love for creating according to specifications from his father, who was a cabinetmaker in Paris. Yet whatever it was that endowed him with this humility, it thereby enabled him to become the finest portrait sculptor now living—finer than Despiau because he is not caught in an elegant formula, and finer than Maillol because he is more various and alive. The concentration of individual life in Lachaise's heads often reminds one of Houdon, since both of them dramatize a character in action. Yet unlike Houdon, who builds up his heads by pellets applied to a core, Lachaise is a true sculptor, a stonecutter who chisels a block to uncover the head inside, so that the result retains something of the original block's massiveness.

Lachaise is the only sculptor in this country who handles his medium with the assurance of a master experienced in all its possibilities, and too reverent to force them. He has so thoroughly assimilated the lessons of the past that he works healthily in tradition without having to express himself "in the style of" any particular period or artist. He never confuses the possibilities of various media, and so his drawings are not sketches for sculpture, not means to an end, but are ends in themselves and exist in their own right.

In a sense every figure of Lachaise's is a portrait—an individual struggling against a particular fate. He and Rouault seem to be the only two modern artists who strike at the heart of human tragedy—Rouault through the tragic persistence of the spirit, and Lachaise through the no less tragic exaltation of the flesh.

HENRY McBRIDE

From *The New York Sun*, October 26, 1935

THE TAWDRY, ineffective funeral I would not have had otherwise. It was in the tradition. That's the way we buried Melville. That's the way we buried Poe. Greatness would not be greatness if it could be understood generally. Nor do I blame humanity for this poverty of vision nor cry out against God for it. It is merely the way things are.

Yet the word "genius" was uttered. There in a Broadway funeral "parlor" the word got uttered. Gilbert Seldes said it. Gilbert improvised a few words and set them to a note of bitterness. Yet the word "genius" was among them. That word will be remembered later. A great man passed from among us without the benefit of singing choir boys, without incense, without processions. There was no "corruptible" putting on the "incorruptible." There was no one even "weeping for Adonais." A few of us who knew that Gaston Lachaise was great sat there like wooden images in a Eugene O'Neill play and scuttled away the moment the crisp accents of Seldes ceased to be heard, to ruminate on greatness in America—and its recompense.

As far as Lachaise was concerned it might almost be said that of recompenses there were none, for genius is not truly paid with money but with comprehension. Not but that there had been some admirers! There always had been a few. Perhaps the most notable was E. E. Cummings, the poet; himself so slightly acknowledged as to be practically of no use. Then there was Gilbert Seldes and later on Lincoln Kirstein and Edward Warburg.

It was probably due to the influence of the two last named that the astonishing one-man exhibition of the Lachaise sculptures occurred in the Modern Museum last winter, an exhibition so overwhelming in its appeal that you would have thought that the whole world must have succumbed to it; but there were no signs of such a submission. Nothing from the collection was sold, and Lachaise told me himself that about all he got from the affair was my sympathetic account of it in *The Sun*. I do not repeat this boastfully but in despair. Were it not that I know that loftiness of feeling is never lost in this sluggish, unwieldly, careless but delightful old world of ours, and is invariably recognized in the end, I should forever abstain from serious art criticism.

But what a contrast there is between this icy reception of Lachaise's magnificent bronze goddess—I believe it was simply entitled "Standing Woman"—and the feverish interest of the Florentines in the productions of their sculptors in the days of the Renaissance. There was no quarrel here as to where the "Woman" should be publicly placed and worshiped as there was over the Michelangelo "David." There was no attendant mob of geniuses to instantly appraise and put a great value upon the work.

When the "David" was completed, so John Addington Symonds records, a solemn council of the most important artists then resident in Florence convened to consider where the statue should be placed. Opinions were offered by, among others, Cosimo Rosselli, Sandro Botticelli, San Gallo, the architect; the illustrious Leonardo da Vinci, Salvestro, a jeweler; Filippino Lippi, David Ghirlandajo, the painter; Michelangelo, the father of Baccio Bandinelli, the sculptor; Giovanni, the father of Benvenuto Cellini; Giovanni delle Corniole, the gem cutter, and Piero di Cosimo, the painter and later on the teacher of Andrea del Sarto.

What a society that was! They had their human frailties, of course, and the jealousies, backbitings and political maneuverings that the flesh is heir to, but there was no possibility in a time when art was so important that any talent for it should be wasted.

Our Lachaise worked, for the most part, in isolation, continually beset with money difficulties that would have ended the career of any ordinary man before it had begun; and it was not until the present year that he received a commission for a public monument worthy of his immense ability. This was to be a group symbolizing the amalgamation of the races in America, and it was to be placed in Fairmount Park, Philadelphia. The accepted sketch clearly indicated that the work when completed would rank among Lachaise's masterpieces—but the artist was not to live to see the idea realized. It was written that he was to be rejected of men, and so he was. Apparently the idea of the Philadelphia monument came nearer to the idea of "success" than the fates permitted, and so he was hastily snatched from the scene.

"In the 'David,' " so John Addington Symonds said, "Michelangelo first displayed that quality of 'terribilità,' of spirit-quailing, awe-inspiring force, for which he afterward became so famous. The statue imposes, not merely by its size and majesty and might, but by something vehement in the conception."

"Terribilità" is a good word and applicable to Lachaise. It was the thing in him that raised him to the heights. Lachaise alone among the sculptors of this generation is the one whom it is not ridiculous to cite in connection with Michelangelo. He was of that same giant breed. It was his terribilità that made him, if you must have a comparison, larger than the Frenchman Maillol. Maillol is a great sculptor and I admire him without reserve, but the beauty he evokes is pastoral, quiet, soothing, pagan. Lachaise, in the few pieces in which he rose to full stature, was more inflammatory. He was nearer, in class, to Rude than to Maillol. Comparisons are always insidious, and it may be even dangerous for a foreigner to rate Rude above Maillol, but, lovely as Maillol's carvings are, who is there who would exchange them for that one shattering relief of Rude's on the Arc de Triomphe?

Just a year ago, at the time of the Modern Museum's exhibition, Lincoln Kirstein wrote the following:

"One may hope that some really unselfish interests concerned with the fine arts will give Lachaise a commission for an even more important civic or public work. (Mr. Kirstein had been speaking of the Fairmount Park memorial.) Many possibilities suggest themselves. For example, there is no worthy memorial to Thomas Jefferson at the University of Virginia, a project which interests Lachaise intensely. There is no fitting monument to Herman Melville, or to Winslow Homer, or Thomas Eakins. John Reed is unhonored by Harvard College. There is no stone to the memory of Hart Crane, whom Lachaise knew and admired. Lachaise has twenty years or more of work ahead which should be the crowning period of his life. Not to make the fullest use of such a talent would be heartless waste."

But T. S. Eliot dubbed the period "The Waste Land."

Lachaise and Madame Lachaise, Georgetown, Maine, 1920s.

Madame Lachaise, Boston, 1901

CHRONOLOGY

1882 Born in Paris, March 19.

1895 Enters École Bernard Palissy to study sculpture.

1898 Enters the Académie Nationale des Beaux-Arts to study in the Atelier Gabriel Jules Thomas.

1899–1903 Exhibits in the Salon des Artistes. Meets Isabel Nagle (neé Dutaud). Military service.

1904–1905 Leaves the Beaux-Arts. Begins work for René Lalique.

1906 Arrives in Boston, January 13.

1906–1912 In Boston, working for Henry Hudson Kitson.

1912–1913 Leaves Kitson, works independently. Meets Paul Manship and becomes his assistant, carving many neoclassic portraits designed by Manship. Marries Isabel Nagle.

1917 Becomes United States citizen.

1918 First exhibition, Stephan Bourgeois Galleries. "*Elevation*" shown in plaster. Henry McBride praises exhibit.

1920 Second exhibition, Stephan Bourgeois Galleries. E. E. Cummings' first appreciation published in *The Dial*.

1921 Frieze commissioned for the American Telephone and Telegraph Building, New York.

1922 Joins Kraushaar Gallery. Resigns as a Director of the Society of Independent Artists.

1924 Gallatin book *Gaston Lachaise* published.

1927 Exhibition, Alfred Stieglitz' The Intimate Gallery. *Standing Woman*, 1912–1927, cast in bronze. Plaster *Floating Woman* shown.

1928 Exhibition, the Brummer Gallery. National Coast Guard Memorial, Washington.

1931 Reliefs executed for R.C.A. Building, Rockefeller Center.

1932 Large plaster relief for Century of Progress Exposition, Chicago World's Fair. Exhibition, Philadelphia Art Alliance.

1933 *Standing Woman*, 1930–1933, cast in bronze.

1934 Reliefs for International Building, Rockefeller Center, New York. *"La Montagne"* executed in cement.

1935 Receives commission for Fairmount Park, Philadelphia, *Welcoming the People*. Museum of Modern Art retrospective and Catalogue. Lachaise dies, October 17.

1937 Exhibition, Whitney Museum, drawings and sculpture.

1938 Exhibition, Brooklyn Museum, February–April.

1947 Exhibition, M. Knoedler & Company Galleries. Catalogue.

1956 Exhibition, Weyhe Gallery, New York, December 1955–January 1956.

1957 Exhibition, Margaret Brown Gallery, Boston, January–February. *"Dynamo Mother"* first exhibited.

1963–1964 Exhibition, Los Angeles County Museum of Art, Los Angeles, and Whitney Museum of American Art, New York.

1964 Exhibition, Robert Schoelkopf Gallery, New York, portraits.

1965 Exhibition, Felix Landau Gallery, Los Angeles, drawings and sculpture.

1966 Exhibition, Robert Schoelkopf Gallery, New York, drawings and sculpture.

This chronology, and the bibliography which follows, are highly selective, and do not include references to major group exhibitions of sculpture and exhibitions of American art in general in which Lachaise has been represented, newspaper and magazine articles, exhibition reviews, and books and catalogues containing only reproductions of Lachaise's work. The Gaston Lachaise Collection of The Yale University Library, New Haven, Connecticut contains reviews, catalogues and other special material pertaining to the sculptor.

SELECTED BIBLIOGRAPHY

Ames, Winslow, "Gaston Lachaise, 1882–1935," *Parnassus*, v. 8, p. 5, continued April 1936, p. 41.

Bourgeois, Stephan, Preface, *Exhibition of Sculptures and Drawings by Gaston Lachaise*, gallery exhibition catalogue, N.Y., January 31 to February 21, 1920.

Cummings, E. E., "Gaston Lachaise," *The Dial*, v. 68, February 1920, pp. 194–204.

——, "Gaston Lachaise," *Creative Art*, v. 3, August 1928, XXIII–XXVI.

——, "On Lachaise," *Twice a Year*, 10th Anniversary Issue, 1948.

Eglinton, Laura, Exhibition Review, *Art News*, v. 33, February 9, 1935, pp. 3–4.

Gallatin, Albert Eugene, *Gaston Lachaise*, 14 pp. 16 collotype reproductions. E. P. Dutton, N.Y., 1924.

Goodall, Donald B., "Gaston Lachaise 1882–1935," *The Massachusetts Review*, August 1960, pp. 674–684.

——, Bibliography, Chronology and Catalogue Information, *Catalogue*, The Los Angeles County Museum of Art, Los Angeles, 1963, and the Whitney Museum of American Art, N.Y., 1964.

Hartley, Marsden, "Thinking of Gaston Lachaise," *Twice a Year*, no. III-LV, 1939–1940.

Hess, Thomas B., "Gaston Lachaise," *Art News*, v. 45, January 1947, pp. 20–21.

Kirstein, Lincoln, *Gaston Lachaise, Retrospective Exhibition*, catalogue, Museum of Modern Art, 64 pp. 42 illustrations, January 30–March 7, 1935.

——, Essay, *Gaston Lachaise, 1882–1935*, exhibition catalogue, M. Knoedler & Company, 20 pp. 8 illustrations, January 20–February 15, 1947.

Kramer, Hilton, "Lachaise and others; The Orswell Collection," *Arts Yearbook*, 4, 1961, N.Y., pp. 87–100.

Kuh, Katherine, "Lachaise, Sculptor of Maturity," Art Institute of Chicago, Museum *Bulletin*, v. XL, no. 3, March 1946.

Mayor, Alpheus Hyatt, "Gaston Lachaise," *Hound & Horn*, July–September 1932.

McBride, Henry, "A Sculptor of Elemental Rhythms," *New York American*, February 25, 1918.

——, "Modern Art," *The Dial*, v. 82, pp. 530–532. June 1927. March 1928, pp. 262–264. May 1928, v. 84, pp. 442–444.

———, "The Death of Gaston Lachaise," *New York Sun*, October 26, 1935.

Nordland, Gerald, "Gaston Lachaise," Introduction in exhibition *Catalogue*, the Los Angeles County Museum of Art, Los Angeles, 1963, and the Whitney Museum of American Art, N.Y., 1964.

Pach, Walter, "Les Tendances Modernes aux États-Unis," *L'Amour de l'Art*, v. 3, January 1922, p. 30.

Rosenfeld, Paul, "Habundia," *The Dial*, v. 81, pp. 215–219. September 1926.

Seldes, Gilbert, "Hewer of Stone," *New Yorker* (Profile), April 4, 1931, pp. 28–31.

Wonders, Anne, "Gaston Lachaise," *Critique*, January–February 1947.

PUBLIC COLLECTIONS

Sculptures by Gaston Lachaise are in the following public collections:

The Museum of Modern Art, New York, New York
The Whitney Museum of American Art, New York, New York

Addison Gallery of American Art, Andover, Massachusetts
Albright-Knox Art Gallery, Buffalo, New York
Arizona State University, Tempe, Arizona
The Art Institute of Chicago, Chicago, Illinois
The Baltimore Museum of Art, Baltimore, Maryland
The Brooklyn Museum, Brooklyn, New York
The Cincinnati Art Museum, Cincinnati, Ohio
The City Art Museum of St. Louis, St. Louis, Missouri
The Cleveland Museum of Art, Cleveland, Ohio
Corcoran Gallery of Art, Washington, D. C.
Dade County Art Museum, Miami, Florida
Des Moines Art Center, Des Moines, Iowa
The Detroit Institute of Arts, Detroit, Michigan
Fine Arts Gallery, San Diego, California
The Fogg Art Museum, Cambridge, Massachusetts
Hackley Art Gallery, Muskegon, Michigan
Honolulu Academy of Arts, Honolulu, Hawaii

Los Angeles County Museum of Art, Los Angeles, California

The Metropolitan Museum of Art, New York, New York

Milwaukee Art Center, Milwaukee, Wisconsin

Minneapolis Institute of Arts, Minneapolis, Minnesota

Munson-Williams-Proctor Institute, Utica, New York

Museum of Art of Ogunquit, Maine

Museum of The City of New York, New York

The Museum of Fine Arts, Boston, Massachusetts

Museum of Fine Arts, Springfield, Massachusetts

William Rockhill Nelson Gallery, Kansas City, Missouri

The Newark Museum, Newark, New Jersey

Norton Gallery, West Palm Beach, Florida

The Philadelphia Museum of Art, Philadelphia, Pennsylvania

The Phillips Collection, Washington, D.C.

Portland Museum of Art, Portland, Maine

The Ringling Museum of Art, Sarasota, Florida

The Rochester Memorial Art Gallery, Rochester, New York

Santa Barbara Museum of Art, Santa Barbara, California

Sheldon Memorial Art Gallery, Lincoln, Nebraska

Smith College Museum of Art, Northampton, Massachusetts

The Smithsonian Institution, Washington, D.C.

Toledo Museum of Art, Toledo, Ohio

University of New Mexico, Albuquerque, New Mexico

University of Texas, Austin, Texas

Vassar College, Poughkeepsie, New York

Wadsworth Atheneum, Hartford, Connecticut

Walker Art Center, Minneapolis, Minnesota

Wichita Art Museum, Wichita, Kansas

Williams College, Williamstown, Massachusetts

Worcester Art Museum, Worcester, Massachusetts

Yale University Art Gallery, New Haven, Connecticut

Examples of Lachaise's work are included in numerous important private collections such as the collections of Joseph H. Hirshhorn, Mrs. Culver Orswell, Nelson A. Rockefeller and Edward M. M. Warburg.

LIST OF WORKS ILLUSTRATED

(Dimension given is height of sculpture.)

1, 2 LOVERS. 1908–1910. Bronze, 4½ inches.

3 DANCING WOMAN. Undated. Gilded Bronze, 10⅞ inches.

4 NUDE WITH COAT. Circa 1912. Plaster, 10¾ inches.

5 STANDING WOMAN. 1910. Plaster, 11⅛ inches.

6 "LA FORCE ETERNELLE." 1917. Bronze, 12½ inches.

7 RECLINING WOMAN. Circa 1917. Plaster, 10⅞ inches.

8 NUDE DANCING. Circa 1917. Gilded Bronze, 14½ inches.

9 IDEAL HEAD. 1921–1923. Bronze, 5½ inches.

10 HEAD. 1922. Nickel-plated Bronze, 3 inches.

11 AMERICAN TELEPHONE AND TELEGRAPH FIGURE. 1921–1923. Plaster, size unknown.

12, 13, 14 STANDING WOMAN called "ELEVATION." 1912–1927. Bronze, 70 inches.

15 BUST of "ELEVATION." Circa 1927. Bronze, 14½ inches.

16 STANDING NUDE. No Date. Plaster, 8 inches.

17 SMALL DRAPED TORSO. No Date. Plaster, 6¾ inches.

18, 19 TORSO of "ELEVATION," 1912–1927. Bronze, 44 inches.

20 "EGYPTIAN HEAD." 1923. Bronze, 13½ inches.

21 WALKING WOMAN. 1922. Polished Bronze, 19 inches.

22 SEATED WOMAN. 1918. Bronze, 12½ inches.

23, 24 STANDING NUDE. 1921. Bronze, 11¾ inches.

25 SEA LION. 1917. Bronze, 11 inches.

26, 27 RECLINING NUDE. 1920–1924. Plaster, 4¼ inches.

28, 29 TWO FLOATING NUDE ACROBATS. 1922. Bronze, 12 inches.

30, 31 "THE MOUNTAIN." 1924. Bronze, 7¾ inches.

32 RECLINING WOMAN, WITH RIGHT ARM RAISED. Circa 1924. Bronze, 13¾ inches.

33 FLOATING NUDE FIGURE. 1924. Bronze, 13 inches.

34, 35 HEAD OF A WOMAN. 1923. Bronze, 10¼ inches.

36 STANDING NUDE, LEFT HAND RAISED. 1927. Bronze, 11¾ inches.

37 TORSO. 1928. Bronze, 9¼ inches.

38, 39, 40 FLOATING FIGURE. 1927. Bronze, 5¾ inches.

41 SLEEPING GULL. 1927. Bronze, 4⅛ inches.

42 STANDING WOMAN, WITH PLEATED SKIRT. 1926. Bronze, 15¾ inches.

43 MALE TORSO. 1928. Bronze, 7¾ inches.

44 WOMAN ON A COUCH. 1928. Bronze, 9¼ inches.

45 "CLASSIC" TORSO. 1928. Plaster, 10¾ inches.

46 E. E. CUMMINGS. 1924. Bronze, 13¾ inches.

47 MARIANNE MOORE. 1924. Bronze with Gold Patina, 14⅞ inches.

48, 49 BEE, RADIATOR CAP. 1924. Chromium-plated Bronze, 3¼ inches.

50, 51 TURKEY, RADIATOR CAP. 1924. Brass, 4 inches.

52 FLOCK OF SEAGULLS. 1924. Bronze, 22¼ inches.

53, 54 DOLPHIN FOUNTAIN. 1924. Bronze, 18 inches.

55, 56 TORSO. 1928. Bronze, 9½ inches.

57 HAND OF RICHARD BUHLIG. 1928. Bronze, 20½ inches.

58 JOHN MARIN. 1928. Painted Plaster, 12 inches.

59 HENRY McBRIDE. 1928. Plaster, 14 inches.

60 EDGARD VARÈSE. 1928. Plaster, 16½ inches.

61 BURLESQUE FIGURE. 1930. Bronze, 24½ inches.

62 TORSO. 1930. Bronze, 13½ inches.

63 "DANS LA NUIT." 1935. Plaster, 31 inches.

64, 65 TORSO. 1933. Marble, 11¾ inches.

66 KNEES. 1933. Marble, 19 inches.

67 SEATED WOMAN HOLDING BREASTS. 1931. Bronze, 6¼ inches.

68 TORSO. 1932. Bronze, 9⅝ inches.

69, 70 BOY WITH A TENNIS RACKET. 1933. Bronze, 23 inches.

71 LINCOLN KIRSTEIN. 1932. Plaster, 15½ inches.

72 KNEELING WOMAN. 1932–1934. Bronze, 19½ inches.

73 "PASSION." 1932–1934. Bronze, 25¾ inches.

74, 75, 76 STANDING WOMAN. 1932. Bronze, 88 inches.

77, 78, 79 TORSO. 1934. Plaster, 45 inches.

80 TORSO WITH ARMS RAISED. 1935. Bronze, 37 inches.

81, 82, 83 "LA MONTAGNE." 1934. Concrete, 60 inches.

84 "IN EXTREMIS." Circa 1934. Plaster, 14 inches.

85, 86 "DYNAMO MOTHER." 1933. Bronze, 10¼ inches.

THE SCULPTURE

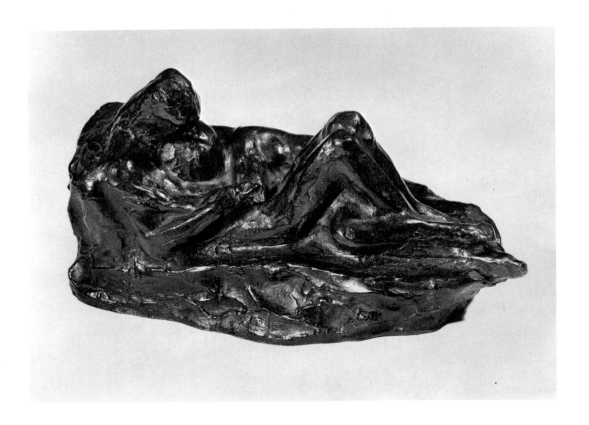

1 LOVERS. Front view. 1908–1910. Bronze, 4½ inches. Lachaise Foundation.

This early sketch presents a theme Lachaise used in one of his last monumental works (Illustration 63).

2 LOVERS. Back view.

3 DANCING WOMAN. Undated. Gilded Bronze, 10⅞ inches.
Collection Mrs. C. O. Wellington, New York, New York.

Personal conception here emerges through art nouveau conventions
of drapery and coiffure. The woman on her toes presages his first
major work, "Elevation" (Illustration 12).

4 NUDE WITH COAT. Circa 1912. Plaster, 10¾ inches.
Lachaise Foundation.

Exhibited in the Armory Show of 1913.

5 STANDING WOMAN. 1910. Plaster, 11⅛ inches.
Lachaise Foundation.

6 *"LA FORCE ETERNELLE."* 1917. Bronze, 12½ inches.
Smith College Museum of Art, Northampton, Massachusetts.

7 RECLINING WOMAN. Circa 1917. Plaster, 10⅞ inches.
Lachaise Foundation.

8 NUDE DANCING. Circa 1917. Gilded Bronze, 14½ inches.
Lachaise Foundation.

9 IDEAL HEAD. 1921–1923. Bronze, 5½ inches.
Addison Gallery of American Art,
Phillips Academy, Andover, Massachusetts.

A model for the head of Illustration 11.

10 HEAD. 1922. Nickel-plated Bronze, 3 inches.
Collection John B. Pierce, Jr., Boston, Massachusetts.

11 AMERICAN TELEPHONE AND TELEGRAPH FIGURE.
1921–1923. Plaster, size unknown.

Destroyed, this was a model for a proposed heroic figure to be executed
in marble and to be placed in the lobby of the Telephone and Telegraph
Building on Lower Broadway. A decorative marble frieze by Lachaise, 60
feet in length, surmounts the lobby.

12 **STANDING WOMAN** called "ELEVATION." 1912–1927. Bronze, 70 inches. Albright-Knox Gallery, Buffalo, New York, James G. Forsyth Fund.

Lachaise's first life-size figure.

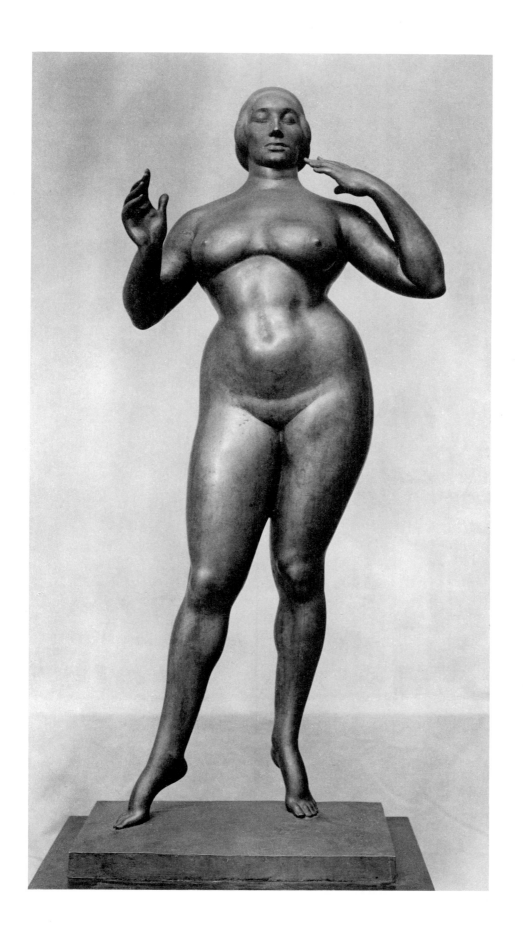

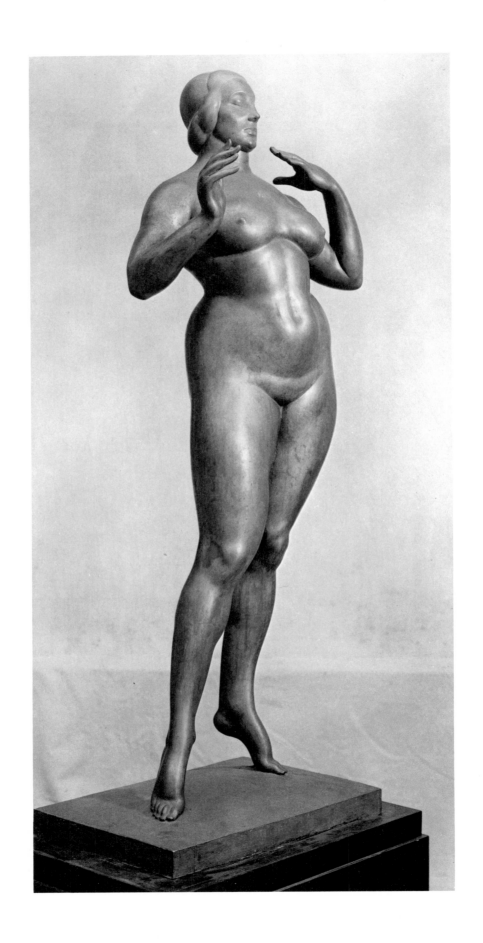

13 "ELEVATION." Side view.

14 "ELEVATION." Back view.

15 BUST of "ELEVATION." Circa 1927. Bronze, 14½ inches.
Collection Mr. and Mrs. T. Edward Hanley, Philadelphia, Pennsylvania.

16 STANDING NUDE.
   No Date. Plaster, 8 inches.
   Lachaise Foundation.

17 SMALL DRAPED TORSO.
   No Date. Plaster, 6¾ inches.
   Lachaise Foundation.

18 TORSO of "ELEVATION." Back view. 1912–1927. Bronze, 44 inches. Lachaise Foundation.

19 TORSO of "ELEVATION." Front view.

20 "EGYPTIAN HEAD." 1923. Bronze, 13½ inches.
Lachaise Foundation.

21 WALKING WOMAN. 1922. Polished Bronze, 19 inches.
Lachaise Foundation.

22 SEATED WOMAN. 1918. Bronze, 12½ inches.
Lachaise Foundation.

23 STANDING NUDE. Back view. 1921. Bronze, 11¾ inches.
Lachaise Foundation.

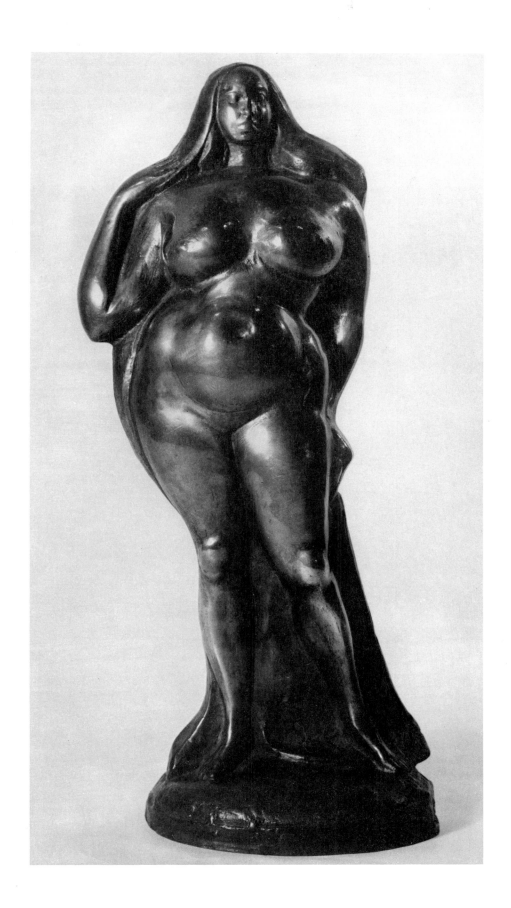

24 STANDING NUDE. Front view.

25 SEA LION. 1917. Bronze, 11 inches.
The Phillips Collection, Washington, D. C.

26 RECLINING NUDE. Back view. 1920–1924. Plaster, 4¼ inches.
Lachaise Foundation.

27 RECLINING NUDE. Front view.

28 TWO FLOATING NUDE ACROBATS. Back view. 1922. Bronze, 12 inches.
Collection Mr. and Mrs. John S. Schulte, New York, New York.

This is one of several sculptures using the same figures differently arranged.

29 TWO FLOATING NUDE ACROBATS. Front view.

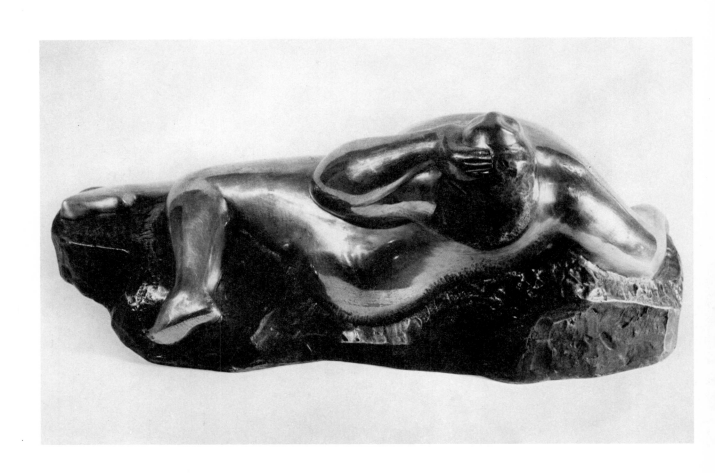

30 "THE MOUNTAIN." Back view. 1924. Bronze, 7¾ inches
Lachaise Foundation.

Lachaise created numerous reclining "Mountain" figures in vary-
ing sizes in stone and bronze—the first in 1913, the last and larg-
est at the end of his life in 1934.

31 "THE MOUNTAIN." Front view.

32 RECLINING WOMAN, WITH RIGHT ARM RAISED.
Circa 1924. Bronze, 13¾ inches. Lachaise Foundation.

33 FLOATING NUDE FIGURE. 1924. Bronze, 13 inches.
Lachaise Foundation.

A small-scale study for the large Floating Figure (Illustration 38).

34 HEAD OF A WOMAN. Side view. 1923. Bronze, 10¼ inches.
Lachaise Foundation.

35 HEAD OF A WOMAN. Front view.

36 STANDING NUDE, LEFT HAND RAISED.
1927. Bronze, 11¾ inches. Lachaise Foundation.

37 TORSO. 1928. Bronze, 9¼ inches.
  Lachaise Foundation.

38 FLOATING FIGURE. 1927. Bronze, 51¾ inches.
The Alcoa Collection of Contemporary Art.
Presently located in Philadelphia, Pennsylvania.

39 FLOATING FIGURE. Back view.

40 FLOATING FIGURE. Front view.

41 SLEEPING GULL. 1927. Bronze, 4⅛ inches.
Lachaise Foundation.

42 STANDING WOMAN, WITH PLEATED SKIRT.
1926. Bronze, 15¾ inches. Lachaise Foundation.

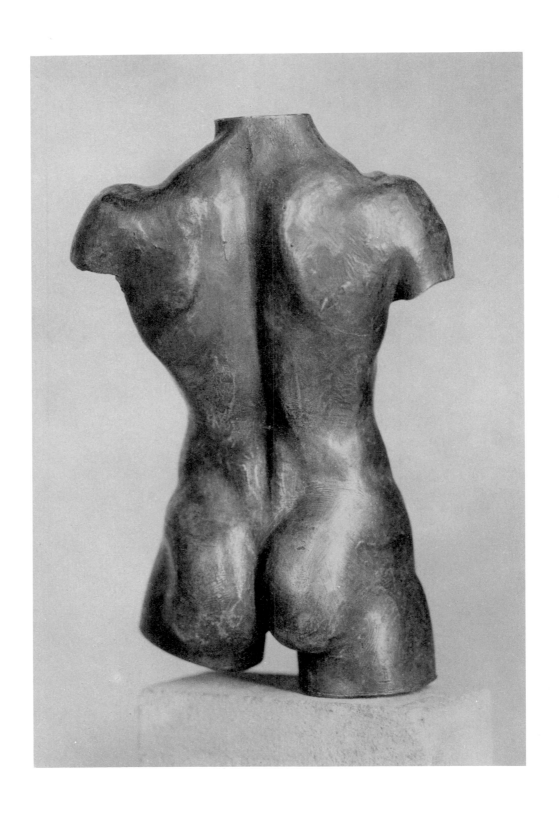

43 MALE TORSO. 1928. Bronze, 7¾ inches.
Collection Mr. and Mrs. Chaim Gross, New York, New York.

44 WOMAN ON A COUCH. 1928. Bronze, 9¼ inches.
Lachaise Foundation.

45 "CLASSIC" TORSO. 1928. Plaster, 10¾ inches.
Lachaise Foundation.

46 E. E. CUMMINGS. 1924. Bronze, 13¾ inches.
Collection Mrs. E. E. Cummings, New York, New York.

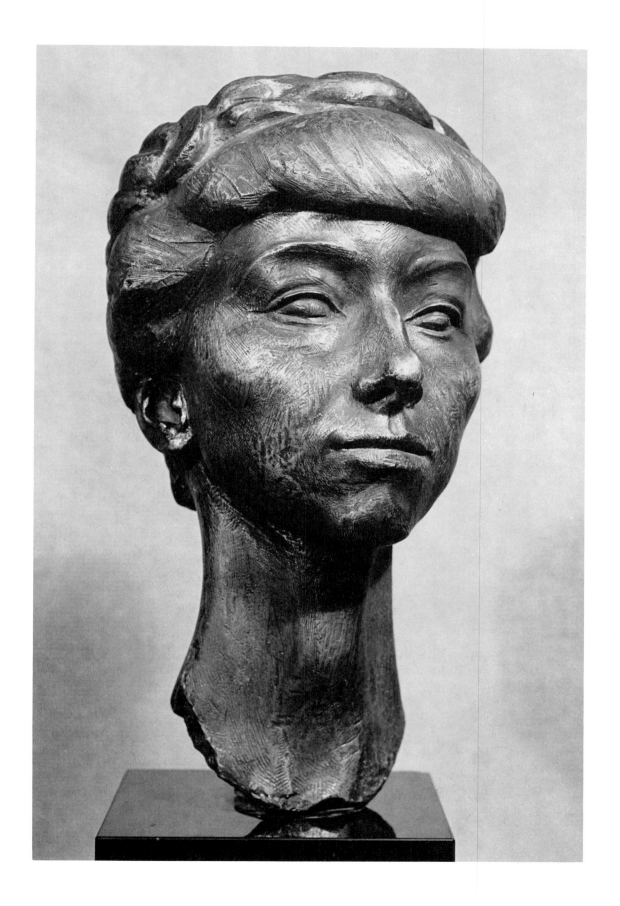

47 MARIANNE MOORE. 1924. Bronze with Gold Patina, 14⅞ inches.
The Metropolitan Museum of Art, New York, New York.
Gift of Lincoln Kirstein, 1959.

48 BEE, RADIATOR CAP. Front view. 1924.
Chromium-plated Bronze, 3¼ inches.
Philadelphia Museum of Art, Philadelphia, Pennsylvania.

50 TURKEY, RADIATOR CAP. Side view. 1924.
Brass, 4 inches.
Lachaise Foundation.

49 BEE, RADIATOR CAP. Side view.

51 TURKEY, RADIATOR CAP. Front view.

52 FLOCK OF SEAGULLS. 1924. Bronze, 22¼ inches.
Collection Mr. Joseph H. Hazen, New York, New York.

53 DOLPHIN FOUNTAIN. Front view. 1924. Bronze, 18 inches.
Collection Whitney Museum of American Art, New York, New York.

54 DOLPHIN FOUNTAIN. Back view.

55 TORSO. Front view. 1928. Bronze, 9½ inches.
Lachaise Foundation.

56 TORSO. Back view.

57 HAND OF RICHARD BUHLIG. 1928. Bronze, 20½ inches.
Collection Mr. and Mrs. Carter Burden, New York, New York.

58 JOHN MARIN. 1928. Painted Plaster, 12 inches.
Lachaise Foundation.

59 HENRY McBRIDE. 1928. Plaster, 14 inches.
Lachaise Foundation.

60 EDGARD VARÈSE. 1928. Plaster, 16½ inches.
Lachaise Foundation.

61 BURLESQUE FIGURE. 1930. Bronze, 24½ inches.
Lachaise Foundation.

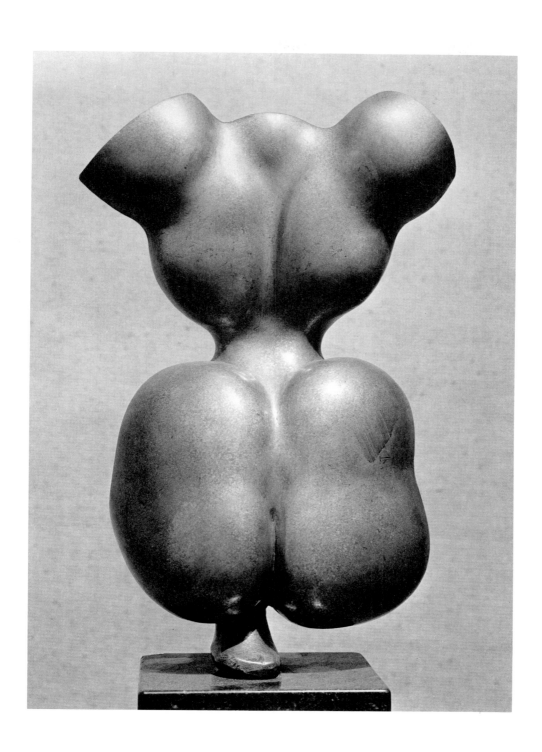

62 TORSO. 1930. Bronze, 13½ inches.
Lachaise Foundation.

63 "DANS LA NUIT." 1935. Plaster, 31 inches.
Lachaise Foundation.

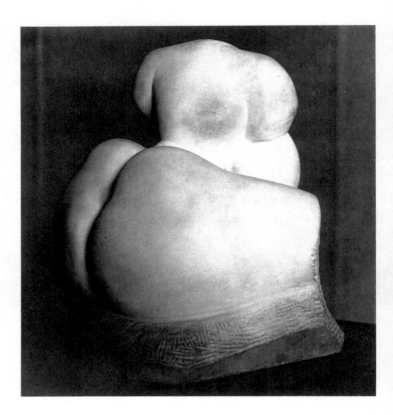

64 TORSO. Front view. 1933. Marble, 11¾ inches.
Smith College Museum of Art, Northampton, Massachusetts.

65 TORSO. Back view.

66 KNEES. 1933. Marble, 19 inches.
Collection The Museum of Modern Art, New York, New York.
Gift of Mr. and Mrs. Edward M. M. Warburg, New York, New York.

67 SEATED WOMAN HOLDING BREASTS. 1931. Bronze, 6¼ inches.
Lachaise Foundation.

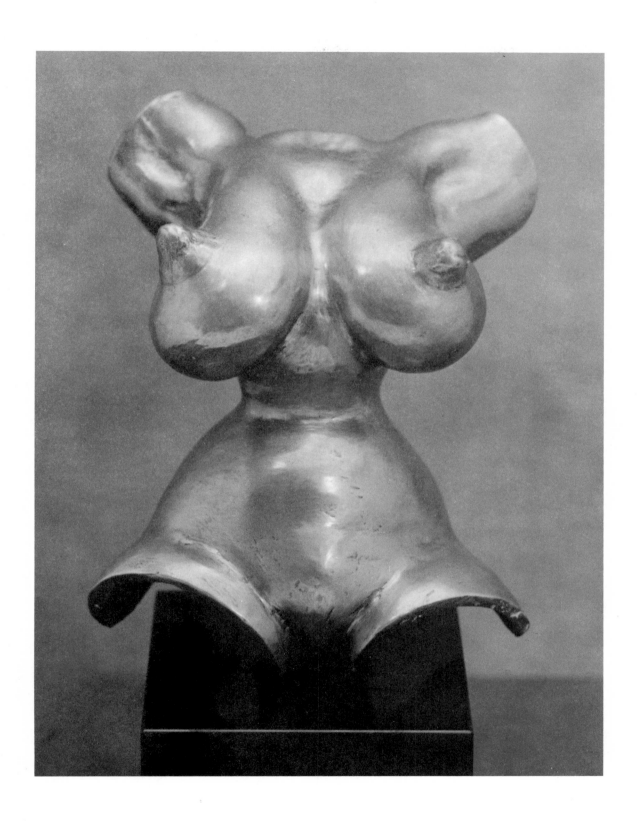

68 TORSO. 1932. Bronze, 9⅝ inches.
   Lachaise Foundation.

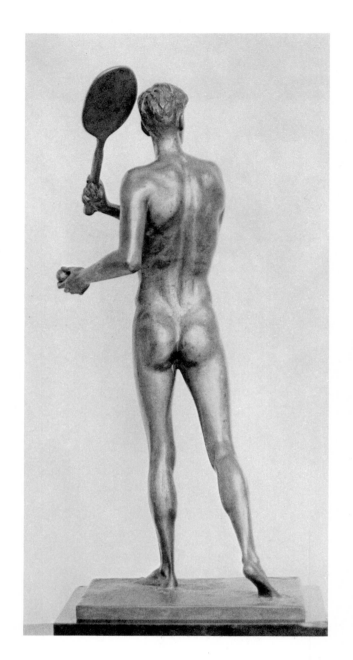

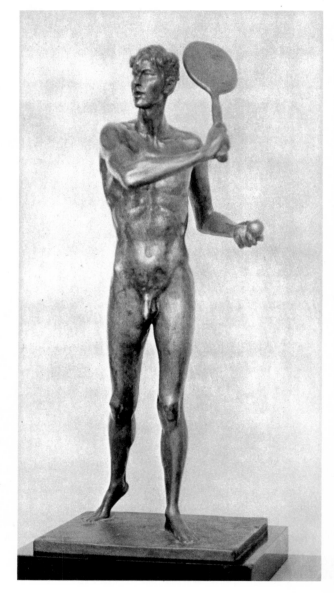

69 BOY WITH A TENNIS RACKET. Back view. 1933. Bronze, 23 inches.
Collection Mr. George L. K. Morris, Lenox, Massachusetts.

70 BOY WITH A TENNIS RACKET. Front view.

71 LINCOLN KIRSTEIN. 1932. Plaster, 15½ inches.
Lachaise Foundation.

72 KNEELING WOMAN. 1932–1934. Bronze, 19½ inches.
Lachaise Foundation.

73 "PASSION." 1932–1934. Bronze, 25¾ inches.
Lachaise Foundation.

74 STANDING WOMAN. Front view. 1932. Bronze, 88 inches.
The Brooklyn Museum, Brooklyn, New York.

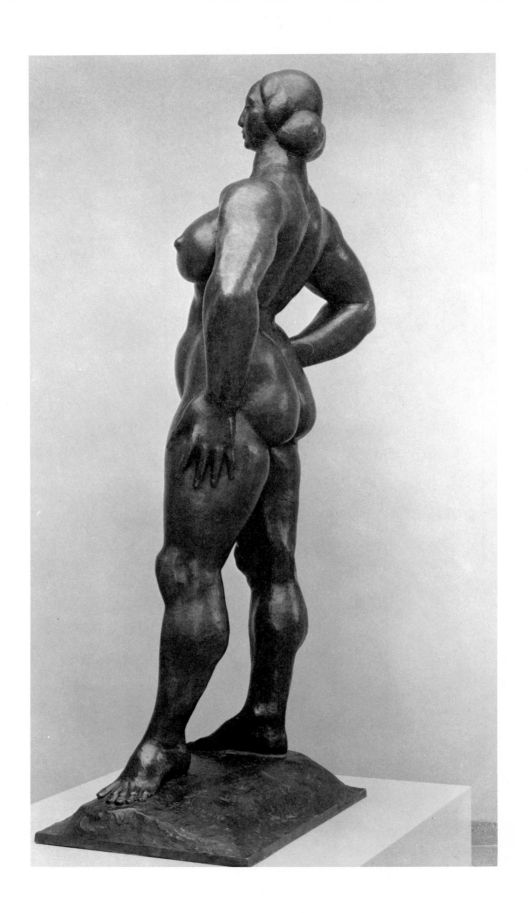

75 STANDING WOMAN. Side view.

76 STANDING WOMAN. Three-quarter view.

77 TORSO. Back view.

78 TORSO. Three-quarter view.

79 TORSO. Front view. 1934. Plaster, 45 inches.
Collection The Museum of Modern Art, New York, New York.
Gift of Mr. Edward M. M. Warburg.

80 TORSO WITH ARMS RAISED. 1935. Bronze, 37 inches.
Lachaise Foundation.

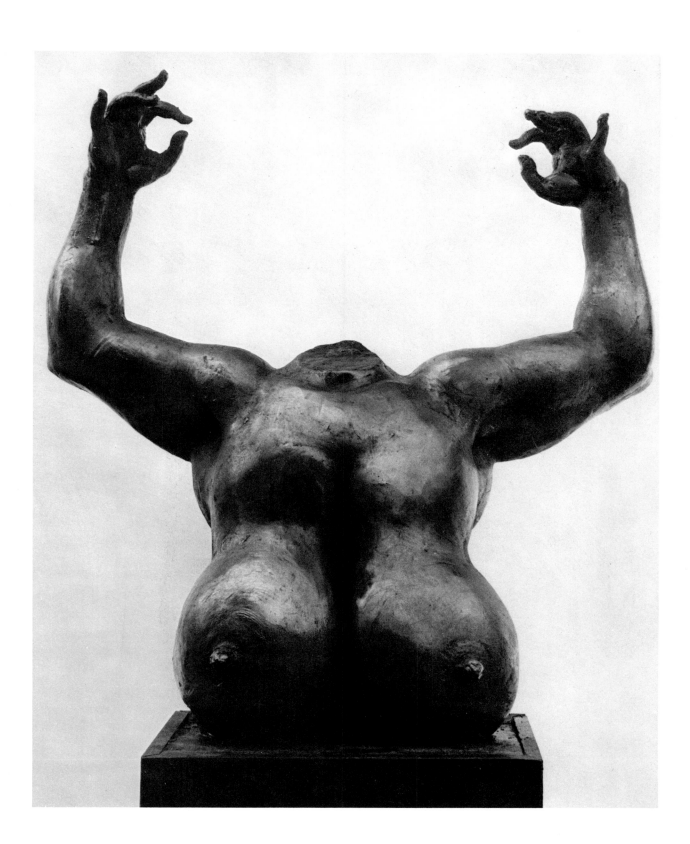

81 "LA MONTAGNE." Front view. 1934. Concrete, 60 inches.
Collection Mr. George L. K. Morris, Lenox, Massachusetts.

82 "LA MONTAGNE." Back view.

83 "LA MONTAGNE." Three-quarter view.

84 "IN EXTREMIS." Circa 1934. Plaster, 14 inches. Lachaise Foundation.

85 "DYNAMO MOTHER." Back view. 1933. Bronze, 10¼ inches.
Lachaise Foundation.

86 "DYNAMO MOTHER." Front view.

PHOTOGRAPH CREDITS

Photographs are by John D. Schiff, New York, except for: Joe Alper, Schenectady, 69, 70, 82, 83; Andover Art Studio, Andover, 9; Brooklyn Museum, Brooklyn, 74, 75, 76; Sherwin Greenberg, McGranahan & May, Inc., Buffalo, 12, 13, 14; Peter A. Juley & Son, New York, 25, 52, 53, 54, 63; Charles P. Mills & Son, Philadelphia, 38, 39, 40; The Museum of Modern Art, New York, 66, 77, 78, 79; O. E. Nelson, New York, 20, 41; Allison Spence, Northampton, 6, 64, 65; Soichi Sunami, New York, 47.

DESIGNED BY EDITH McKEON

COMPOSITION BY THE STINEHOUR PRESS

PRINTED BY THE MERIDEN GRAVURE COMPANY

BOUND BY RUSSELL–RUTTER